EXPLORING FEELINGS

Cognitive Behaviour Therapy To Manage ANGER

DR. TONY ATTWOOD

EXPLORING FEELINGS: Cognitive Behaviour Therapy To Manage ANGER

All marketing and publishing rights guaranteed to and reserved by

721 W. Abram Street
Arlington, Texas 76013
800-489-0727
817-277-0727
817-277-2270 (fax)
E-mail: info@futurehorizons-autism.com
www.FutureHorizons-autism.com

ISBN 1-932565-21-3

TABLE OF CONTENTS

INTRODUCTION

Overview of the Exploring Feelings program

The Cognitive Behaviour Therapy program Exploring Feelings was designed by the author to be highly structured, interesting and successful in encouraging the cognitive control of emotions. Every child participating in the program has a workbook for the six two-hour sessions that includes activities and information to explore the specific feelings of being happy, relaxed, anxious or angry. There are sections in the workbook to record individual comments and responses to questions. At the end of each session, a project is explained to the child, which is to be completed before the next session. At the start of the next session the project is discussed with the person implementing the program or the group of participants using the program. The Exploring Feelings program is designed to explore the mental world from a scientific perspective. There are two Exploring Feelings programs, one is designed to explore and manage anxiety, the other to explore and manage anger.

The original program was designed for small groups of two to five children between the ages of 9 and 12 years, with two adults conducting the program. However, the Exploring Feelings program can easily be modified so that it can be used with just one child. The activities can also be modified to be age appropriate for an adolescent or adult. The program was designed as a treatment for an anxiety disorder or anger management problem in children with Asperger's syndrome but the program can be equally applied to children with High Functioning Autism and Pervasive Developmental Disorder, Not Otherwise Specified (PDDNOS). The author also designed the program so that it does not have to be implemented by a qualified psychologist. A teacher, speech pathologist, occupational therapist or parent could implement the program without having training in Cognitive Behaviour Therapy.

The first session of the program explores two positive emotions, happiness and relaxation, with a range of activities to measure, experience and compare positive emotions in specific situations. The second session is an exploration of the feelings of anxiety or anger and recognition of the changes that occur in physiology, thinking, behaviour and speech. The concept of a toolbox with different types of tools to 'fix the feeling' is explained, with a focus on physical tools that provide a constructive release of emotional energy (e.g., going for a run or bouncing on the trampoline), and relaxation tools that lower the heart rate (e.g., listening to music or reading a book). In session three, social tools are explored; for example, how other people can help restore positive feelings through words and gestures of reassurance and affection or how avoiding social contact (solitude) can be one of the most effective emotional restoratives for children and adults with

Asperger's syndrome. Also explored in session three are thinking tools, a category of activities or thoughts that test the reality and probability of feared or frustrating situations or outcomes. In session four the program uses the concept of a 'thermometer' as a measuring instrument for the 'temperature' of an emotion. Discussion with the person implementing the program then explores how the child can borrow or share strategies or tools to successfully manage his or her anxiety or anger. In session five Social Stories™, originally developed by Carol Gray, are adapted to be a means of improving social and emotional knowledge and strategies for emotion management. Session five also includes the concept of creating an 'antidote' to poisonous or negative thoughts. In the final session, the child or children work on designing a Cognitive Behaviour Therapy program for themselves and (if the program is being used in a group context) other members of the group, to improve the management of anxiety or anger. The course also includes a before and after program activity or test, to demonstrate the child's increase in knowledge and ability to manage emotions.

Introduction To Cognitive Behaviour Therapy

Research studies, clinical experience and autobiographies have confirmed that individuals with Asperger's syndrome have considerable difficulty with the understanding and expression of emotions and are at risk of developing an anxiety disorder or problems with anger management. However, we are only just beginning to learn how to modify effective psychological treatments such as Cognitive Behaviour Therapy (CBT) for children and adults with Asperger's syndrome.

Asperger's syndrome and related conditions such as autism, High Functioning Autism and PDDNOS are considered as part of the Autism Spectrum Disorders (ASD) or Pervasive Developmental Disorders (PDD). The theoretical models of Autism Spectrum Disorders developed within cognitive psychology and research in neuro-psychology provide some explanations as to why such individuals are less able to understand and manage emotions.

Extensive research by cognitive psychologists on Theory of Mind skills, that is, the ability to perceive and understand what someone may be thinking or feeling and the ability to reflect on one's own thoughts, confirms that children and adults with Asperger's syndrome have considerable difficulty identifying and conceptualizing the thoughts and feelings of other people and themselves. The interpersonal and inner world of emotions appears to be uncharted territory for people with Asperger's syndrome. This became the basis of the Exploring Feelings program.

Research on Executive Function and Asperger's syndrome suggests characteristics of being disinhibited and impulsive with a relative lack of insight that affects general functioning. Impaired Executive Function can also affect the cognitive control of emotions. Clinical experience indicates there is a tendency to react to emotional cues without careful thought or cognitive reflection.

Research using new neuro-imaging technology has also identified structural and functional abnormalities of the amygdala of subjects with an ASD or PDD such as Asperger's syndrome. The amygdala is a part of the brain known to regulate a range of emotions including anger, fear and sadness. Thus we also have neuro-anatomical evidence that suggests there will be problems with the perception and regulation of emotions.

Modifications to Conventional Cognitive Behaviour Therapy (CBT)

CBT has been developed and refined over several decades and, using rigorous scientific evaluations, proven to be effective in changing the way a person thinks about and responds to feelings such as anxiety, sadness and anger. CBT focuses on aspects of cognitive deficiency in terms of the maturity, complexity and efficacy of thinking about emotions, and cognitive distortion in terms of dysfunctional thinking and incorrect assumptions. Thus, it has direct applicability to children and adults with Asperger's syndrome who are known to have deficits and distortions in thinking about thoughts and feelings. The cognitive deficits can include an immaturity in the expression of emotions, especially affection and anger, a limited vocabulary of subtle emotional expressions and a lack of efficacy in terms of a range of appropriate emotional repair mechanisms. The cognitive distortion can include a misunderstanding of someone's intentions, especially whether an act was deliberate or accidental, a tendency to make a literal interpretation of what someone says or does, and dysfunctional reasoning.

Cognitive Behaviour Therapy programs for children and adults with Asperger's syndrome has several stages, the first stage being affective education, with the participants learning about emotions. It includes discussion and exercises on the connection between cognition or thoughts, affect or feelings and behaviour and the way in which individuals conceptualize emotions and perceive various situations. Affective education can also provide tuition and encouragement of maturity and subtlety in emotional response in specific situations. The subsequent stage is cognitive restructuring, and includes a schedule of activities to practice new cognitive skills. Cognitive restructuring corrects distorted conceptualizations and dysfunctional beliefs. The participants are encouraged to establish and examine the evidence for or against their thoughts or emotions and create a new perception of specific events. A graded schedule of activities is also developed to allow the participants to practice new abilities.

Affective Education

The main goal of affective education is to learn why we have emotions, their use and misuse and the identification of different levels of expression. A basic principle is to explore one emotion at a time as a theme for a project. A useful starting point is happiness or pleasure. The program Exploring Feelings describes, and the children discover, the salient cues that indicate a particular level of emotional expression in facial expression, tone of voice, body language and context. The face is described as an information center for emotions. The typical errors include not identifying which cues are relevant or redundant, and misinterpreting cues. The person implementing the program uses a range of games and resources to 'spot the message' and explain the multiple meanings: for example, a furrowed brow can mean anger or bewilderment; loud voice does not automatically mean that the person is angry.

Once the key elements that indicate a particular emotion have been identified, it is important to use an 'instrument' to measure the degree of intensity. The person implementing the program can construct a model 'thermometer' and use a range of activities to measure the level of expression. These may include pictures that illustrate different levels of emotional expression or words on cards that describe the intensity of emotion; each picture or word may then be placed at the appropriate point on the thermometer. During the program it is important to ensure the child and person implementing the program share the same definition or interpretation of words and gestures and to clarify any confusion. Another value of using a thermometer is to help the child perceive his or her 'early warning signals' - the rising of emotional temperature - that indicate emotional arousal that may need cognitive control.

When one or two positive emotions and the levels of expression are understood, the next component of affective education is to use the same procedures for a contrasting negative emotion such as anxiety or anger. When exploring negative emotions such as anxiety and anger, activities are used to explain the concept of fight or flight as a response to perceived danger or threat. The children explore how such emotions affect their bodies and thinking, such as increasing heart rate, and changes in body chemistry (adrenalin), perspiration, muscle tone, perception and problem solving ability. Over many thousands of years, these changes have been an advantage in anxiety-provoking or threatening situations. However, in our modern society, we can have the same intensity of fight or flight reaction to what we imagine or misperceive as a worry or threat. It is also important to explain that when we are emotional, we can be less logical and rational and this affects our problem solving abilities and decision-making. To be calm and 'cool' will help the child in both interpersonal and practical situations.

Cognitive Restructuring

Cognitive restructuring enables the child or adult to correct distorted conceptualizations and dysfunctional beliefs. The process involves challenging the person's current thinking with logical evidence and ensuring the rationalization and cognitive control of emotions. The first component is to establish the evidence for a particular thought or belief. People with Asperger's syndrome can make false assumptions of the intentions of others, especially in terms of an action being deliberate or accidental, and have a tendency to make literal interpretations. A casual comment may be taken out of context or to the extreme or the person may not recognize the comment was meant to be a joke.

Comic Strip Conversations

To explain an alternative perspective or to correct errors or assumptions, Comic Strip Conversations (CSC) can help the child discover the thoughts, beliefs, knowledge and intentions of the participants in a given situation. Comic Strip Conversations were originally developed by Carol Gray (1998) and have been adapted by the author as an invaluable part of CBT for children and adults with Asperger's syndrome. The technique involves drawing an event or sequence of events in story board form with stick figures to represent each participant and speech and thought bubbles to represent their words and thoughts. The speech bubbles can be drawn in a variety of ways to convey emotion - for example, sharp edges to indicate anger or wavy lines to indicate anxiety. Colors can also be used, with the child making the choice of which color represents a specific emotion. Happy or positive statements could be written in green (the choice of color is determined by the child) while unpleasant thoughts could be written in red. A whole color chart can be developed; for example embarrassed comments may be written with a pink marker, or sad feelings written in blue. The color and tone can then be translated into relevant aspects of the person's tone of voice or body language. As the child writes in the speech or thought bubbles, the choice of color indicates his or her perception of the emotion conveyed or intended. A Comic Strip Conversation can clarify the child's interpretation of events and the rationale for his or her thoughts and response. Subsequent guidance using a CSC can help the child identify and correct any misperception and to determine how alternative responses will affect someone's thoughts and feelings. Comic Strip Conversations allow the child to analyse and understand the range of messages and meanings that are a natural part of conversation or play. The speech and thought bubbles, as well as choice of colors, can illustrate the hidden messages.

The author and Carol Gray have found that children with Asperger's syndrome often assume that the other person is thinking exactly what they are thinking; or they assume other people think exactly what they are saying, and nothing else. The Comic Strip Conversations can then be used to show that each person may have very different thoughts and feelings in the same situation. Another advantage of this technique is that it can be used to represent the sequence of events in a conversation and illustrate the potential effects of a range of alternative comments or actions.

One common effect of the misinterpretation of another person's intention, whether it was deliberate or accidental, is the tendency to be overly suspicious or almost paranoid. Our knowledge of impaired Theory of Mind skills in the cognitive profile of children and adults with Asperger's syndrome suggests a simple explanation. Others will know from the context, body language and character of the person involved that the intent was not to cause distress or injury. However, individuals with Asperger's syndrome may focus primarily on the act and the consequences to themselves—he hit me and it hurt so it was deliberate—while others would consider the circumstances; he is a nice guy, was running, tripped and accidentally knocked into me.

The child with Asperger's syndrome may have a limited repertoire of responses to situations that elicit anxiety or anger. The person implementing the program and child create a list of appropriate and inappropriate responses and the consequences of each option. Various options can be drawn as a flow diagram that enables the child to determine the most appropriate response in the long term. Another part of cognitive restructuring is to actually challenge certain beliefs with facts and logic. Information can be provided that establishes that the statistical risk of a particular event is highly unlikely and not necessarily fatal, such as being struck by lightning; or when another child says, "I'm going to kill you," does he really have a murderous intention?

The author has developed the Emotional Toolbox, a successful strategy for cognitive restructuring that is one of the main activities to help repair a feeling in the CBT program Exploring Feelings.

The Emotional Toolbox

From an early age, children will know a toolbox contains a variety of different tools to repair a machine or fix a household problem. The strategy used in Exploring Feelings is to identify different types of 'tools' to fix the problems associated with negative emotions, especially anxiety and anger. The range of tools can be divided into those that quickly and constructively release or slowly reduce emotional energy and those that improve thinking. The person implementing the program works with the child or adult with Asperger's syndrome, and his or her family to identify different tools that help fix the feeling as well as some tools that can make the emotions or consequences worse. The participants use paper and pens during a brainstorming session in which they draw a toolbox and pictures and descriptions of different types of tools and activities that can encourage constructive emotion repair.

Physical tools

A hammer can represent tools or actions that physically release emotional energy. A picture of a hammer is drawn on a large sheet of paper and the child or participants in the program suggest safe and appropriate physical activities. For young children this may include going for a run, bouncing on the trampoline or going on a swing. For older children and adults, sports practice and dancing may be used to 'let off steam' or release emotional energy. For example, a child nominated a game of tennis as one of his physical tools as it 'takes the fight out of me'. Other activities include cycling, swimming and playing the drums. Some household activities can provide a satisfying release of potentially destructive energy without expensive repairs; for example, recycling, where cans or packaging are crushed, or old clothes are torn up to make rags, can be a useful tool to repair feelings of frustration. Kitchen activities can include squeezing oranges or pounding meat. Adults may consider some aspect of gardening or household renovations.

Some children and adults with Asperger's syndrome may have already identified that destruction is a physical tool that is a very effective 'quick fix' to end the unpleasant feeling, but have not been careful in choosing the focus of their physical release. If something is to be broken to release stress, then it is preferable that the energy is channelled into a constructive activity. The author uses the term 'creative destruction' to describe some recycling activities that effectively release energy.

Relaxation tools

Relaxation tools help to calm the person and lower the heart rate. A paintbrush could be used to illustrate this category of tools, and activities could include drawing, reading and listening to music. People with Asperger's syndrome often find that solitude is their most relaxing activity. They may need to retreat to a quiet, secluded sanctuary as an effective emotional repair mechanism. Young children may relax by using gentle rocking actions and engaging in a repetitive action: this can include manipulating an object such as a stress ball that has the same soothing qualities as an adult manipulating worry beads.

Other relaxing activities can include massage, a brief doze or sleeping as well as relaxation activities that have been practiced beforehand that focus on breathing and imagery. For adults, a routine chore such as making the house clean and tidy can be a repetitive action that results in satisfaction and relaxation when complete. Obviously there are problems if this is the predominant tool in the toolbox, as it could become the focus for an Obsessive-Compulsive Disorder. Teachers may also use specific chores in the classroom. For example, a teacher who notices that a child is becoming distressed, may suggest a high status responsibility that will enable the child to leave a situation, or may distract the child with an activity that restores order and consistency, such as leaving the class to take an important message or document to the school office, or tidying the book cupboard and placing all the books in alphabetical order. An adult with Asperger's syndrome may nominate his or her own relaxation tools for use at work and at home.

Social tools

This group of tools uses other people as a means of managing feelings. The goal is to find and be with someone (or an animal or pet) who can help change the mood. The social activity will need to be enjoyable and without the stress that can sometimes be associated with social interaction, especially when interacting with more than one other person (remembering the description, 'two's company, three's a crowd'). Those with Asperger's syndrome often prefer to avoid crowds.

The supportive social contact can include seeking and being with someone who genuinely admires or loves the child or adult, gives compliments and manages to say the right things to repair the feelings. This can be a family member - perhaps a grandparent who has time to be patient with the child - or a friend. Communication using Internet chat lines can be a successful social activity that can be an emotional repair mechanism. People with Asperger's syndrome may have greater eloquence and insight in disclosing their thoughts and feelings by typing rather than talking. One does not need skills with eye contact and reading a face or changes in vocal tone or body language when engaged in a 'conversation' on the Internet. The chat line can include other people with Asperger's syndrome who have genuine empathy and may offer constructive suggestions to repair a mood or situation. The author has known several mature adults with Asperger's syndrome who have provided wise support and advice for younger members of the 'Asperger community' using the Internet.

Sometimes the best friend may be a pet. Despite the negative mood or stressful events of the day, dogs are delighted to see their owner, show unconditional adoration and clearly enjoy the person's company, as demonstrated by the wagging tail. Time spent in the company of animals can be a very effective emotional restorative for children and adults with Asperger's syndrome.

A tool or activity that may help to repair negative emotions is to help someone or to be needed - an altruistic act. The author has noted that some children, and especially adults, with Asperger's syndrome can change their mood from negative introspection to positive enthusiasm when helping others. This can include activities such as helping someone who has difficulties in an area of the child's talents or expertise: for example, helping an adult negotiate or fix a problem with a computer, or guiding another classmate who does not have the child's ability with a subject such as mathematics. Adults with Asperger's syndrome can enjoy and benefit emotionally from volunteer work, particularly with the elderly, very young children and animals. Being needed and appreciated is a significant emotional repair mechanism for all of us, and also those with Asperger's syndrome.

Thinking tools

The child can nominate another type of implement, such as a screwdriver or wrench, to represent a category of tools that can be used to change thinking or knowledge. The child is encouraged to use his or her intellectual strength to control feelings using a variety of techniques. Self-talk can be used, such as, 'I can control my feelings' or, 'I can stay calm,' when under stress. The words can be reassuring and encourage self-esteem. Evan, a young man with Asperger's syndrome, was discussing thinking tools with the author and created the strategy of making an 'antidote to poisonous thoughts.' The procedure is to provide a comment that neutralizes or counterbalances negative thoughts. For example, the thought, 'I can't do it' (poisonous thought) can be neutralized by the antidote, 'Asking for help is the smart way to fix it.' It is necessary to determine the person's negative or poisonous thoughts in a particular situation and create a personalized antidote that is remembered or written on a card to be carried by the person and 'administered' or remembered when needed.

Another thinking tool is to put the event in perspective: a reality check. The approach is to use logic and facts with a series of questions such as, 'Is there another shop where we could buy that computer game?' or 'Will children teasing you about your interest in astronomy prevent you from being a successful astronomer?'

Children and adults with Asperger's syndrome have a great motivation to acquire knowledge, and a special type of 'thinking tool' is to create a project on the topic that has become associated with anxiety. For example, a person with an Autism Spectrum Disorder could perceive the sound of a vacuum cleaner as unbearably intense. The project can include exploring the value and functions of a vacuum cleaner, dismantling an old vacuum cleaner to discover how it works and being reassured that it will be switched off once the carpet is cleaned of dust and debris. There can be a comparison of different types of vacuum cleaners, and an exploration of which ones have a more tolerable noise, using the thermometer to measure the intensity of the feeling. The author has noted that some special interests of children with Asperger's syndrome actually began in association with a feared sensory experience as an intelligent way of reducing fear. For example, a fear of the sound of a flushing toilet became an interest in plumbing systems for several children, and the sudden and intense sound of thunder became the basis of a special interest in weather systems to predict when a thunderstorm was likely.

One thinking tool that can be used by children with Asperger's syndrome to improve mood and self-esteem is achieving academic success, which is often not the choice of other children. When children with Asperger's syndrome are agitated, the teacher may instruct them to complete a school activity that they enjoy and for which they have a natural talent, such as solving mathematic problems or spelling. Other children would probably try to avoid academic tasks when stressed.

Cue controlled relaxation is also a useful thinking tool. The strategy is for the child to have an object in their pocket that symbolizes relaxation, or to which through classical conditioning or association, they respond by feeling relaxed. For example, a teenage girl with Asperger's syndrome was an avid reader of fiction, her favorite book being *The Secret Garden*. She kept a key in her pocket to metaphorically open the door to the secret garden, an imaginary place where she felt relaxed and happy. A few moments touching or looking at the key helped her to contemplate a scene described in the book and to relax and achieve a more positive state of mind. Adults can have a special picture in their wallet, such as a photograph of a woodland scene, which reminds them of solitude and tranquillity.

Special interest tools

Children and adults with Asperger's syndrome can experience intense pleasure when engaged in their special interest. The degree of enjoyment may be far in excess of other potentially pleasurable experiences. The child can be encouraged to engage in his or her interest as a means of restoring the emotional equilibrium, a counter balance of pleasure. The activity can sometimes appear to be mesmerizing and dominating all thought but this can effectively exclude negative thoughts such as anxiety and anger. When the child or adult with Asperger's syndrome is very distressed, the most effective emotional restoratives are solitude and becoming totally absorbed in the special interest.

We know that in the general population, routines, rituals and repetition are calming activities and one of the characteristics of the special interests of children and adults with Asperger's syndrome is their repetitive, routine and ritualistic nature. An adolescent with Asperger's syndrome, known to the author, had a great interest in Japanese culture and performed the elaborate and ritualized tea ceremony whenever she felt anxious. The activity was clearly very soothing for her. Luke Jackson (2002), a teenager with Asperger's syndrome, describes the cataloging of the examples of his interests as a means of 'personal defrag'. The activity creates a sense of enjoyment, comfort and security.

In behavioral learning theory terms, the repetitive action, thought or special interest becomes a form of negative reinforcement; it is a powerful form of reinforcement because it ends an unpleasant feeling. The author has noted that the degree of motivation and duration of time spent on the interest is proportional to the degree of anxiety or agitation. The more the person experiences worries, confusion and agitation, the more the interest becomes obtrusive, dominant or bizarre. If the child or adult with Asperger's syndrome has few means of enjoyment and relaxation, what may have started as a source of pleasure and tranquillity, under conditions of extreme stress can become a compulsive act reminiscent of an Obsessive Compulsive Disorder. This problem can occur when the child has very few tools in his or her emotional toolbox. If the special interest is the only source of relaxation or mental escape, then it can become irresistible. Being prevented from achieving uninterrupted access to such a powerful emotional restorative creates even more stress. A program of controlled or timed access can be introduced to ensure the time spent on the interest is not excessive. Unfortunately, from the child's point of view, time goes quickly when you are enjoying yourself. There may need to be some negotiation and compromise regarding the duration of access. The special interest can, therefore, be a powerful but potentially psychologically dangerous tool in the toolbox.

...loring Feelings program can make changes to the program in ...n each activity, but also in making adjustments to include the ...or or motivator. For example, an interest in the weather could ...g the thermometer with a barometer and using weather terms ...age girl with Asperger's syndrome who had a special inter-...rnados, was encouraged to use her knowledge of the weath-...n was considered as being in a fog, anxiety as being frozen ...nado was her description of intense pleasure.

...lbox

...of tools that can be included in the toolbox, which may be ...ement that are used in the general population, or unusual ...ts with Asperger's syndrome.

...ildren and adults with Asperger's syndrome to manage ...g clear signs of a diagnosable anxiety disorder or a clin-...d as episodes of intense anger (an agitated and external-...be recommended as a potential emotion management

...rger's syndrome also have signs of Attention Deficit ...der. One of the charac......s of a combination of the two disorders is for the child to react ...pulsively when experiencing emotional arousal. Such children have a tendency to react without cognitive reflection, such as checking if the act was accidental or giving consideration to the consequences of retaliation. A trial of stimulant medication could reduce emotionally impulsive reactions.

Some children with Asperger's syndrome have a fluctuation of emotions that is cyclical. A mood diary can determine the amplitude and wavelength of any cyclical pattern. The caregiver or person with Asperger's syndrome can nominate the degree of anxiety or anger experienced in the day using a numerical rating system based on the concept of an emotion thermometer. If the person felt somewhat serene and tolerant during most of the day, the score may be zero to one, while a predominant feeling of anxiety or anger is measured at the upper end of the scale, perhaps nine or ten. The mood diary can be used to examine whether there are any cyclical characteristics indicative of a bipolar disorder or moods related to hormonal fluctuations. The administration of medication could achieve a reduction in amplitude so that the person with Asperger's syndrome does not experience the extremes of negative emotions.

The author suggests that the management of anger can be conceptualized as the management of destructive energy, and antipsychotic medication can reduce the person's energy levels. The medication is prescribed as a sedative, rather than treatment for clear signs of schizophrenia. As a matter of expediency, and often in the absence of CBT, such medication may be necessary to maintain the person's circumstances and reduce the intensity of explosive and destructive emotional energy.

Clinical experience has confirmed the value of medication for the treatment of anxiety and anger but there are some concerns, often voiced by parents and those with Asperger's syndrome. One concern of parents and physicians is that at present we do not have longitudinal studies of the long-term effect of using psychotropic medication on young children. Another concern, for parents, teachers and especially the child and adult with Asperger's syndrome is the effect on the person's clarity of thought. Many children and adults with Asperger's syndrome report that medication slows his or her thinking and cognitive skills. People with Asperger's syndrome often value their clarity of thought: one adult with Asperger's syndrome described his reaction to medication: 'It was like I was locked out of my own home.'

Other tools

Other potential tools for the toolbox are enjoyable activities such as watching a favourite comedy. Children with Asperger's syndrome can enjoy humor typical of their developmental level and be remarkably creative with their own puns and jokes or unique sense of humor. Sometimes a good laugh can be a very effective emotional restorative. Another tool is to read the autobiographies of adolescents and adults with Asperger's syndrome for encouragement and advice. We now have several autobiographies written by children and adults with Asperger's syndrome, which can be remarkably inspirational.

Another category of tools, which could be described as sensory tools, involves the assessment of the person's ability to cope with the sensory world and identifying strategies to avoid specific sensory experiences. For example, the position of the child's desk in class or the adult's workstation may be changed, and if necessary moved, to reduce the general level of noise, light intensity and proximity to aromas such as cleaning products. Sensory Integration therapy or the use of Irlen lenses can reduce the distress caused by aspects of hypersensory perception that is a characteristic of Asperger's syndrome.

Another tool that can encourage self-control is the suggestion of a prize or reward. The reward can be to earn access to preferred activities, the special interest or even money. The author has noted that some children with Asperger's syndrome are natural capitalists. The subsequent problem can be economic inflation.

A tool that can be used for some children, especially girls, with Asperger's syndrome, is to act like a person they know or admire who could cope with the situation. In high school, speech and drama classes can be used to practice and role-play what to do and think in specific situations. Some teenagers with Asperger's syndrome, and especially girls, have used drama training and acting abilities to achieve social success. An example of this is Liane Holiday Willey whose autobiography is titled "Pretending to be Normal" (Holiday Willey 1999).

The concept of a toolbox can also be used in group activities to compare the effectiveness of the tools used by different participants in the group, with the possibility of 'borrowing' a tool used by someone in the group, a family member or friend. The author has noted that an interesting and extremely valuable by-product of the toolbox strategy is that it can teach children and adults with Asperger's syndrome how to repair not only their own emotions, but those of their family members and friends.

Inappropriate Tools

The program Exploring Feelings includes a discussion of inappropriate tools (with the comment that one would not use a hammer to fix a computer) in order to explain how some actions, such as violence, thoughts of suicide and engaging in retaliation are not appropriate tools or emotional repair mechanisms. For example, one child known to the author would slap himself to stop negative thoughts and feelings. Another tool that could become inappropriate is the retreat into a fantasy world. The use of escape into fantasy literature and games can be a typical tool for ordinary adolescents but is of concern when this becomes the dominant or exclusive coping mechanism and the border between fantasy and reality becomes unclear, leading to concern regarding the development of signs of schizophrenia. The person implementing the program also needs to consider whether teenagers or adults with Asperger's syndrome are using illegal drugs and alcohol to manage their stress levels and mood, and whether prescription medication would be more effective, legal and safer. Other inappropriate tools could include taking their stress out on someone, self-injury and the destruction of something valuable or precious.

It is also necessary to evaluate tools used by parents, family members and teachers and to remove from the toolbox those that may be inappropriate or counter-productive. Children and adults with Asperger's syndrome are often confused by certain emotions and this can be the case with the expression of affection. They may fear what they do not easily understand and affection from others may not be effective as an emotional repair mechanism. A hug could be perceived as an uncomfortable squeeze. Sometimes, affection can be the cause of more agitation or confusion. A teenage boy with Asperger's syndrome was describing how sometimes he feels very sad but said, 'But I get angry when someone tries to cheer me up,' and a younger child who has Asperger's syndrome, when asked if a hug would help when he was upset, replied with an emphatic, 'No, I get madder.'

Parents, friends, family members and teachers will need to be aware that affection is a very powerful emotional restoration tool for themselves but not necessarily for children and adults with Asperger's syndrome. Demonstrating affection could 'add fuel to the fire.' The person implementing the program may need to explain to those with Asperger's syndrome why other people respond to their distress with gestures and words of affection. This can reduce their confusion and increase their tolerance of affectionate behavior in others. However, sometimes affection can be used as an emotion repair mechanism or tool in the toolbox but the level of expression may be much less demonstrative than would be used with someone who does not have Asperger's syndrome.

Unusual tools

Unusual responses to emotions are also a characteristic of Asperger's syndrome and considered in the program Exploring Feelings. The person with Asperger's syndrome may laugh when expected to cry and show tears. Crying and laughing are both tension release mechanisms; unfortunately, the person with Asperger's syndrome may not know or be able to recognize which release mechanism is appropriate for the social context.

The author explored another unusual response during a group session on sadness; a teenage girl with Asperger's syndrome explained that, 'Crying doesn't work for me, so I get angry.' Clinical experience suggests that tears may be rare as a response to feeling sad, with a more common response being anger, which may be a more effective emotional restorative for those with Asperger's syndrome. In such instances, the program will need to include an explanation as to why some reactions are misinterpreted by others and to enable others to understand why they do not see the expected tears.

Clinical experience with the concept of an emotional toolbox has provided some interesting comparisons between children with Asperger's syndrome and typical children who naturally have a much wider range of tools, the most popular and effective being social tools. For children with Asperger's syndrome, physical acts are often the first tool to be employed, to quickly and effectively discharge the emotion. Emotion management is usually achieved by actions rather than reflection and relaxation. Children with Asperger's syndrome often need active encouragement to use other people as a constructive and effective means of repairing their feelings.

Social Stories™

Another cognitive restructuring activity included in Exploring Feelings is a technique developed by Carol Gray called Social Stories™, which is remarkably effective in enabling the child to understand the cues and responses for specific social and emotional situations. Preparing Social Stories™ also enables others to understand the perspective of the child, and why his or her social behavior can appear unduly confused, anxious, aggressive or disobedient. Carol Gray (2004) has recently revised the criteria and guidelines for writing a Social Story™ and the following is a brief summary of the guidelines that can be used when writing a Social Story™ as part of the Exploring Feelings program.

A Social Story™ describes a situation, skill or concept in terms of relevant social cues, perspectives and common responses in a specifically defined style and format. The goal is to share accurate social and emotional information in a reassuring and informative manner that is easily understood by the child (or adult) with Asperger's syndrome. The first Social Story™ and at least 50 per cent of subsequent Social Stories™ should describe, affirm and consolidate existing abilities and knowledge and what the child does well. This can avoid the problem of a Social Story™ being only associated with failure. Social Stories™ can also be written as a means of recording achievements in using new knowledge and strategies. It is important that the child does not exclusively associate Social Stories™ with his or her ignorance or social and emotional failure.

One of the essential aspects of writing a Social Story™ is to collaboratively determine how a particular situation is perceived by the person with Asperger's syndrome, abandoning the assumption that the adult knows all the facts, thoughts, emotions and intentions of the child with Asperger's syndrome. The structure of the story comprises an introduction that clearly identifies the topic, a body that adds detail and knowledge and a conclusion that summarizes and reinforces the information and any new suggestions. The story or text is written from a first or third person perspective. For younger children, the first person perspective, using the personal pronoun 'I,' provides the child with information that can be personalized and internalized. For teenagers and adults, the Social Story™ can be written in the third person perspective, 'he or she,' with a style resembling an age appropriate magazine article. The term Social Story™ may then be changed to Social Article. If the person has a special interest, the person implementing the Exploring Feelings program can incorporate the interest in the text. For example, if the child has a special interest in the sinking of the Titanic, then scenes from the film or personal recollections in history books or documentaries can be used to illustrate and emphasize some of the key information in the Social Story™. Drawings, pictures and photographs can also illustrate the text of the Social Story™.

Social Stories™ use positive language and a constructive approach. The suggestions are what to do rather than what not to do. The text will include descriptive sentences that provide factual information or statements but one of the reasons for the success of Social Stories™ is the use of, to use Carol Gray's term, perspective sentences. These sentences are written to explain a person's perception of the physical and mental world. Perspective sentences describe thoughts, emotions, beliefs, opinions, motivation and knowledge. They are specifically included to improve Theory of Mind abilities. Carol Gray recommends including cooperative sentences to identify who can be of assistance, which can be a very important aspect of emotion management, and directive sentences that suggest a response or choice of responses in a particular situation. Affirmative sentences explain a commonly shared value, opinion or rule, the reason why specific codes of conduct have been established and why there is the expectation of conformity. Control sentences are written by the child to identify personal strategies to help remember what to do. Carol Gray has developed a Social Story™ formula such that the text describes more than directs. The Social Story™ will also need a title, which should reflect the essential characteristics or criteria of a Social Story™. Further training on how to write Social Stories™ can be achieved by completing the Writing Social Stories™ program (Gray 2000).

After writing the Social Story™, other people in the child's every day world will need to know how they can help the child successfully implement the new knowledge and strategies. The child may create a Social Stories™ book or folder to keep the stories as a reference book at home or school, and have copies of some Stories that may be kept in a pocket or a wallet to read again in order to refresh his or her memory just before or during a situation when the Social Story™ may be needed.

Research Evidence on the Effectiveness of Exploring Feelings

The author and Kate Sofronoff of the University of Queensland in Australia have conducted two studies to examine the effectiveness of the Exploring Feelings program to reduce reported levels of anxiety and anger. Both studies used a randomized controlled trial of the program in children diagnosed with Asperger's syndrome. The first study examined the Exploring Feelings program for anxiety management. Sixty-five children aged 10 to 12 years were recruited to participate in the study. Measures were taken on three occasions, pre-intervention, immediately post-intervention and at six-week follow-up. Two forms of the intervention were compared, one in which only the children participated but parents were given written materials, and a second in which parents were taught all strategies and information in the same manner as the children. The two intervention groups were compared with a wait-list control group. The Exploring Feelings program was implemented by postgraduate clinical psychology students at the University of Queensland in Brisbane, Australia, using groups of three children and two psychologists.

The first measure, 'James and The Math Test,' was completed by the child and was developed specifically for the study. Each child was asked to generate strategies for 'James' to cope with his anxiety in the situation outlined in the story. The scoring system for James and the Math Test was one point for each positive strategy generated. At the end of the study, the analysis of the results confirmed a significant improvement across time in the two intervention groups in the ability to generate strategies, compared with the wait-list control group. The second measure in the study was a parent-report measure of child anxiety. The third measure was a parent-report measure gauging the level of social worry experienced by the child. The results using the two parent report measures demonstrated that the Exploring Feelings program was effective in reducing anxiety symptomatology with a significant reduction in parent-rated symptoms from pre-intervention to six-week follow-up, both on the total score and on individual subscales. A parental measure of self-efficacy in the management of typical behaviour problems also showed significant improvement in the two intervention groups. Parental feedback about the program was generally very positive but significantly more positive in the second intervention in which they were more actively included.

While conducting intervention trials it is often not possible to capture or even to hypothesize some of the findings in a quantitative medium. As part of the evaluation of the program, the authors of the study asked parents to describe any changes in their child, either positive or negative, that they felt could be attributed to their participation in the program. Many parents pointed to the development of friendships among their children. Some parents also noted that the children seemed more confident in their day-to-day interactions and suggested that the time spent with children similar to themselves, and with very positive therapists, had helped in this respect. Other parents reported that, while issues still arose on a regular basis for their child, they found that the children were slower to become distressed and quicker to recover from distress, especially if they could be encouraged to use strategies that they had learned. Interestingly, most of the children participating in the program enjoyed attending the university each week and many children were quite dismayed when the program ended. The paper on the study using the Exploring Feelings program for anxiety management has been accepted for publication in 2005 (Sofronoff and Attwood, in press).

The second study, also conducted by the author and Kate Sofronoff examined the effectiveness of the Exploring Feelings program for anger management. Forty-five children aged 10 to 14 years with a diagnosis of Asperger's syndrome were randomly allocated into an experimental or wait-list control group. The presence of problems with anger management was established using a parent and child interview. As in the previous study, postgraduate clinical psychology students implemented the program. In the intervention condition children were assigned to pairs and each pair worked through the program with two psychologists. Parents were placed together to form a 'parent group' and a psychologist worked through the components of each session with them, at the same time as the child sessions were taking place.

The first measure, 'Dylan is being Teased' was completed by the child and was developed specifically for the study to measure the ability to generate appropriate anger management strategies. This and all other measures were administered at pre-intervention, post-intervention and at the 6-week follow-up. The child completed a questionnaire about his or her own anger issues and parents completed a monitoring measure for the week prior to commencing the program. Parents were asked to note the number of instances of anger that occurred in the child each day. Parents were also asked to rate on a scale of 1 to 10 how confident they felt in managing their child's anger. Parents were also asked to indicate how confident they felt their child was in managing his or her own anger using the same rating scale. Parents also completed a standardized inventory of anger.

Preliminary analysis of the results of the study clearly indicates that the number of anger episodes reported by parents decreased significantly over time and that this was maintained at follow-up. Parents further described an increase in their own confidence in managing anger in their child that was maintained at follow-up and a perception that the child had more confidence in his or her own ability to manage anger. The standardized measure of anger also showed a significant decrease over time for the intervention group. The paper on the study of the Exploring Feelings program for anger management is still in preparation before submission to a research journal.

Further information can be obtained from the author at anthonyattwood@compuserve.com

References

Gray, C.A. (1998) 'Social Stories™ and Comic Strip Conversations with students with Asperger Syndrome and High-Functioning Autism.' In Schopler, E., Mesibov, G. and Kunce, L.J. (eds) *Asperger's Syndrome or High-Functioning Autism* New York: Plenum Press.

Gray, C. A. (2000) *Writing Social Stories™ with Carol Gray.* Arlington, Future Horizons.

Gray, C. A. (2004) Social Stories™ 10.0 *Jenison Autism Journal.* 15, 2-21.

Social Stories 10.0: The New Defining Criteria and Guidelines, Jenison Autism Journal, Vol. 15, #4, pp. 2-21, Jenison Public Schools, Jenison, MI.

Holliday Willey, L. (1999) *Pretending to be Normal: Living with Asperger's Syndrome.* London: Jessica Kingsley Publishers.

Jackson, L. (2002). *Freaks, Geeks and Asperger Syndrome: A User Guide to Adolescence.* London: Jessica Kingsley Publications.

Sofronoff, K. and Attwood, T (in press) A Cognitive Behaviour Therapy Intervention for Anxiety in Children with Asperger's Syndrome *Journal of Child Psychology and Psychiatry.*

EXPLORING FEELINGS
Cognitive Behaviour Therapy To Manage ANGER

— SESSION 1 —

1) Introduction of participants

A. My favorite

Food _____

Drink _____

Schoolwork _____

TV Program _____

Sport _____

Book _____

Hero _____

B. Strengths and Talents

Everyone has strengths and talents. My strengths and talents are activities that I do well or enjoy. Some of these are:

_____

_____

_____

_____

_____

_____

_____

C. Place a check next to your strength or talent

❏ Reading

❏ Spelling

❏ Handwriting

❏ Computers

❏ Mathematics

❏ History

❏ Science

❏ Creative

❏ Facts about _____ (Fill in your favorite topic)

❏ Construction toys

❏ Dolls

❏ Understanding animals

❏ Imagination

❏ Knowledge

❏ Being a friend

❏ _____

❏ _____

D. What is good about my

Body - my physical qualities

_____

_____

_____

_____

_____

Thinking - my intellectual qualities

_____

_____

_____

_____

_____

Character - The type of person I am

_____

_____

_____

_____

_____

E. If you have a special interest, that is something you know about almost as an expert, what is it?

_____

_____

_____

_____

_____

_____

2) Being Happy

Our moods change all the time. One mood we enjoy is feeling happy. We are now going to explore the feeling of happiness.

A. When do you feel especially happy?

_____

_____

_____

_____

_____

_____

B. What can you imagine that would make you feel happy?

_____

_____

_____

_____

C. How do we know we are happy?

How does your face look?

_____

_____

What thoughts do you have?

_____

_____

How are your energy levels?

_____

_____

How do you move your body?

_____

_____

How does your voice change?

_____

_____

D. Rope Game (Part 1)

Stand on the length of rope that represents how happy you would feel in these situations? One end of the rope represents not very happy, the other end is very happy. The choice of where to stand is up to you.

1. You are allowed to have the day off school.

2. You get an A for a school assignment.

3. You are invited to a birthday party.

4. You find and can keep $20.00.

5. Your mother says that she loves you.

E. Rope Game (Part 2)

Place the following words that describe the different levels of happiness at the position on the rope that measures the strength of the feeling.

Happy	Thrilled	Delighted
Proud	Ecstatic	Satisfied
Hopeful	Joyful	Pleased
Merry	Loving	Cheerful
Enthusiastic	_____	_____

3) Feeling Relaxed

A. Another feeling is being relaxed.

There are some words that express different levels of relaxation. As in the previous game, where would you place each word on the rope?

Calm	Content	Peaceful
Safe	Comfortable	Quiet
Relaxed	Cool	Secure
Resting	Easy	Soft
Tranquil	Familiar	Serene

_____   _____   _____

B. How does your body show that you are feeling relaxed?

What happens to your:

Heart _____

_____

Breathing _____

_____

Posture _____

_____

Speech _____

_____

Movement _____

_____

Thinking _____

_____

Gestures _____

_____

C. When do you feel relaxed and why does it help you feel relaxed?

_____

_____

_____

_____

D. Relaxation Practice

Physical method using breathing and muscles.

Thinking methods using imagination and self-talk.

4) Explanation of the project.

Projects for Session 1

Things to be happy about:

In my room

_____

_____

_____

_____

In my home

_____

_____

_____

_____

My family

_____

_____

_____

_____

My friends

_____

_____

_____

_____

Me

_____

_____

_____

_____

Computers

_____

_____

_____

_____

Weekends

_____

_____

_____

_____

Other Things

_____

_____

_____

Happiness Diary

During the next week remember a time when you felt especially happy and why. Did this make anyone else feel happy?

_____

_____

_____

_____

_____

Make a note of when you helped someone feel happy and how you achieved this.

_____

_____

_____

_____

_____

Create a Pleasures Book

Create a scrapbook of the activities, experiences, thoughts and sensations that make you feel happy. Provide a brief explanation of why they make you feel happy. This can include favorite activities and thoughts as well as sensations such as a favorite food, aroma, texture, sound or scene.

Collection of Relaxation Pictures

From magazines and newspapers find and collect some pictures of people who are relaxed and describe why they are relaxed and how relaxed you think they feel from a scale of 1 to 10 with 10 being extremely relaxed.

Create Cue Cards

Create pictures or use photographs of scenes or situations that make you feel relaxed just looking at them. The card needs to be small enough and strong enough to fit in your pocket, for example the size of a credit card. Try to create about three cards.

What makes me angry?

Here is a list of statements describing what makes some people angry. Check the ones that are true for you and how angry it makes you feel from 1 to 10 (with 10 being very angry) and add some of your own that have not been listed.

Statement ....**Rating**

❑ When people talk about me behind my back ....

❑ When I get my work wrong ....

❑ When other people get hurt..

❑ When others won't play with me ....

❑ When I am treated unfairly ....

❑ When I am shouted at...

❑ When people interfere with my games ....

❑ When people stop me doing what I want to .... ☐

❑ When others get more attention than me .... ☐

❑ When people call me names .... ☐

❑ When I am losing at football .... ☐

❑ When people are rude about my family .... ☐

❑ When people bully my friends .... ☐

❑ When someone calls me a liar .... ☐

❑ When someone pushes me .... ☐

❑ When I get told off and others don't .... ☐

❑ When things get broken .... ☐

❑ When someone takes my things .... ☐

❑ When there is a lot of noise and I am trying to concentrate .. ☐

❑ When I have to do something I don't want to do .... ☐

❑ When I am told off in front of my friends .... ☐

❑ When I get interrupted .... ☐

❑ When people don't give me a chance .... ☐

❑ When other people are angry .... ☐

❑ When people don't listen to me .... ☐

❑ When people don't understand me .... ☐

Other things that make me angry are:

1 _____

2 _____

3 _____

Reference: Faupel, Henick and Sharp: Anger Management. David Fulton Publishers: London 1998.

EXPLORING FEELINGS
Cognitive Behaviour Therapy To Manage ANGER

— SESSION 2 —

1) Review main points discovered in session 1

2) Discuss each person's project work

    A. Things to be happy about

    B. Happiness diary

    C. Pleasures book

    D. Relaxation pictures

    E. Cue cards

    F. Feeling anger list

3) Why we feel angry

    A. What happens to our bodies and thinking when we feel angry?

        1. heart rate _____

        2. breathing _____

3. muscles _____

4. posture _____

5. face _____

6. speech _____

7. thinking _____

B. Game: Things that happen when we feel angry.

Decide which of the following are signs or clues of feeling angry.

sweaty palms	wide eyes	cough
lump in throat	runny nose	dry mouth
increased heart beat	falling asleep	burping
crying	muscle tension	sneezing
fast breathing	tingly tummy	goose bumps
gritting teeth	wobbly knees	blushing
flappy hands	chattering teeth	blinking
headache	'shaky' voice	laughing
feeling 'jumpy'	feeling 'dizzy'	needing the toilet
smiling	happy thoughts	being relaxed
yawning	feeling strong	clapping
itchy skin	thinking of hurting someone	making a fist
red face	a frown	breaking things
swear words	staring at someone	loud voice

4) Heroes who become angry

Can you think of a hero in a book, film or television program who has felt angry? When you think of that person, why were they feeling angry and how did they cope with the feeling? What did they do or think that stopped the feeling becoming too strong?

_____

_____

_____

_____

_____

_____

_____

5) A time when I have felt angry

Think of a time or situation when you have felt very angry. Draw a simple outline of yourself on a large piece of paper. On the outline write down the effect on your:

A. heart rate_____

B. breathing_____

C. muscles_____

D. posture _____

E. face _____

F. speech _____

G. thinking —using thought bubbles; you can use several bubbles if you had several thoughts.

Also measure how angry you felt on a scale from 1 (a little bit angry) to 10 (really mad). Then explain how you coped with feeling angry, what did you do or say? Did anyone help you and how did they help you? List those:

_____

_____

_____

_____

_____

6) An Emotional Toolbox to Fix the Feeling

As much as we have a tool box full of different tools to repair a machine, we could imagine another type of tool box to repair some of our feelings. There could be different types of tools in your emotional tool box. One type of tool in a mechanics tool box is a hammer. A hammer could represent physical activities that use lots of energy that can 'repair' feeling angry. Another tool in a tool box is a brush to brush away the dust. This could represent things you can do to help you relax and stay calm.

Projects for Session 2

Think of some physical activities (physical 'tools') or relaxing activities (relaxation 'tools') that you can do to help you feel less angry. On one sheet write the things you already do or could do. For the other sheet, ask members of your family or friends for their ideas or 'tools' and write them down. You may be able to use their ideas or 'borrow their tools'

EXPLORING FEELINGS
Cognitive Behaviour Therapy To Manage ANGER

— SESSION 3 —

1) Review main points discovered in session 2

2) Discuss and share each person's project work:

A. Emotional Tool Box - Physical activities

B. Emotional Tool Box - Relaxing activities

3) An Emotional Tool Box - Part 2

A. Social Tools

How can other people help you fix your feelings?

1. If your friend was feeling angry, how could you help them? Would this work for you too?

_____

_____

_____

2. If your brother/sister/cousin was feeling angry how could you help them?

_____

_____

_____

3. If your mother, father, grandmother or care giver was feeling angry, how could you help them?

_____

_____

_____

4. How could these people help you?

_____

_____

_____

Think of the social tools you could have in your tool box and why they are useful tools when you feel angry.

- who could you talk to, human or animals?

- practice using the social tools

_____

_____

_____

B. Thinking Tools

Thoughts that dissolve angry feelings.

What you could say to yourself.

1. I could put things into perspective by:

_____

_____

_____

2. A reality check might be:

_____

_____

_____

3. I could think of the consequences by:

_____

_____

_____

4. I could use my imagination to:

_____

_____

_____

C. Other Tools

Other things that can help me feel less angry.

1. Special interest.
   How could my hobbies and interests help?

   _____

   _____

   _____

2. Humor may help by:

   _____

   _____

   _____

3. Acting may help by:

   _____

   _____

   _____

D. Inappropriate Tools

What could you do or think that would make the feelings worse?

_____

_____

_____

Projects for Session 3

1. Make your own emotional tool box

2. Between now and next session, when you start to feel a little bit angry try using some of the tools in your tool box. Which tool or tools did you use? Did they work?

_____

_____

_____

_____

_____

_____

_____

_____

EXPLORING FEELINGS
Cognitive Behaviour Therapy To Manage ANGER

— SESSION 4 —

1) **Review main points discovered in session 3**

2) **Discuss each person's emotional tool box, and how they used the 'tools' since the last session.**

3) **Thermometer activity**

A. Stand on the rope which represents a 'thermometer' to measure the degree of anger. Your position should express your degree of anger in each of the following situations:

- When you cannot connect to the internet
- The other children are laughing at you because you got the answer wrong.
- Two boys say that you are stupid.

B. Think of a situation that makes you feel just a little bit angry. What would that situation be?

_____

_____

_____

4) Practice using the emotional tool box to help in the situation you have described.

Projects for Session 4

1. Draw a thermometer on a very large piece of paper, about the size of an open newspaper. Think of the situations that make you feel angry, from just a little bit annoyed to really mad. Write down each situation on a Post-it, and stick each Post-it on the thermometer in the place that represents the degree of anger that you feel.

2. Practice using the emotional tool box to help in the situation that you described on the previous page.
   What happened?

   _____

   _____

   _____

   _____

What did you do?

_____

_____

_____

_____

Were the 'tools' successful?

_____

_____

_____

_____

EXPLORING FEELINGS

Cognitive Behaviour Therapy To Manage ANGER

— SESSION 5 —

1) Review key points discovered in session 4

2) Discuss each person's thermometer and Post-its and review the strategies used, discussed in the previous session.

3) Social Stories™

Choose a situation that makes you feel a little bit more angry and we can write a Social Story™ to help you understand the situation and to feel less angry.

_____

_____

_____

_____

_____

_____

_____

4-A Antidote to poisonous thoughts

In this activity you can create thoughts that act as 'an antidote' to 'poisonous thoughts.' The first activity is to decide whether the following thoughts are an antidote or a 'poison' that will make you feel more angry. Mark **A** (antidote) or **P** (poison), beside each phrase.

I'm a loser.. ☐

They will laugh at me.. ☐

I can stay calm .... ☐

I'll forget what I have to say .... ☐

I'm not good at homework .... ☐

It's not winning, it's enjoying the game .... ☐

I can't get it to work... ☐

Everyone hates me.. ☐

Relaxing makes my thinking better.................................. ☐

I will be better next time... ☐

Good decision.. ☐

I might enjoy a new experience .... ☐

Someone can help me... ☐

I could get hurt .... ☐

Think, then choose .... ☐

Relax, it's not that bad .... ☐

4-B Create a thought that is an antidote to the following 'poisonous thoughts'

1. I always make mistakes

_____

_____

_____

2. I am useless at handball

_____

_____

_____

3. No one will pass me the ball

_____

_____

_____

4. She will break it

_____

_____

_____

5. I can't cope

_____

_____

_____

6. I'm going to hit him

_____

_____

_____

7. They are talking about me

_____

_____

_____

8. You say I did but I didn't do it

_____

_____

_____

Projects for Session 5

1. Write a Social Story™ with your parents about one of the situations that made you feel angry. Then actually use the strategies in the Social Story™ for the real situation.

_____

_____

_____

_____

_____

2. Write a list of your own 'poisonous thoughts' and your own antidotes.

_____

_____

_____

_____

_____

EXPLORING FEELIN

Cognitive Behaviour Therapy To Manage A

— SESSION 6 —

1) Review key points discovered in session 5

2) Discuss each person's Social Story™ and list of antidotes to poisonous thoughts.

3) Sharing Strategies

Choose another situation when you feel angry and briefly describe the situation and how angry you feel on your thermometer.

_____

_____

_____

_____

_____

_____

_____

4) Decide which tools you could use from your tool box.

A. Activity Tools

_____

_____

_____

_____

B. Relaxation Tools

_____

_____

_____

_____

C. Social Tools

_____

_____

_____

_____

D. Thinking Tools

_____

_____

_____

_____

E. Other Tools

_____

_____

_____

_____

5) Write a Social Story™ to help understand the situation and to give you a plan of what to do.

_____

_____

_____

_____

_____

_____

_____

_____

_____

_____

_____

_____

_____

6)   Create thoughts that you can say to yourself that can be an antidote to poisonous thoughts.

_____

_____

_____

_____

_____

_____

_____

EXPLORING FEELINGS
Cognitive Behaviour Therapy To Manage ANGER

— TRAINER'S NOTES —

Central Themes

Session 1—Introduction

Strengths and Talents
Being Happy
Feeling Relaxed

Session 2—Why we feel angry

Heroes who become angry
A time when I have felt angry
An emotional tool box - physical tools
An emotional tool box - relaxation tools

Session 3—Emotional Tool Box

Social Tools
Thinking Tools
Other Tools
Inappropriate Tools

Session 4—Practice using the tool box

Session 5—Social Stories™

Antidote to poisonous thoughts

Session 6—Sharing Strategies

Suggestions for Group Cohesion

Emphasise success and discovery

Be careful with idioms

Acknowledge intelligence

Use the special interest as a metaphor

No right or wrong answers

Ground rules will need to be established at the start of session 1.

One person leads the activity. The other person's function is recording information and maintaining attention.

Dylan is being teased

My friend at school is Dylan. We are in Mrs Smith's class. Dylan is a great friend and we like to do the same things at lunch time. Sometimes we play handball, or go to the library and read about volcanoes, and we both like The Simpsons.

There are three boys in our grade who are not our friends. They like to find someone and tease them and get them into trouble. We don't know why they do it. Sometimes they can be really mean and call you names, which are not true, and want to punch you or push you onto the ground. Dylan and I don't do that to anyone.

Dylan has been in trouble with the Principal for getting mad at them and hitting them. They start it but he gets into more trouble then they do. He was suspended for three days last week when they called him a 'Psycho.' When they said that, he told them to stop, but they didn't, so he hit one of them on the nose. There was a lot of blood everywhere.

On Friday, at lunchtime, they started to tease him again; calling him chicken and saying he is fat and gay. If he gets mad at them again he will be excluded and have to leave the school forever. He is my only friend.

Write down what you could do and say to help Dylan keep cool and not get mad with them.

_____

_____

_____

_____

_____

_____

_____

_____

_____

_____

_____

_____

_____

_____

_____

Session 1

Time	Activity	Resource

10 mins **Dylan is being teased**

Distribute 'Dylan is being teased work sheet' to each participant. Explain to the participants that they will be filling this in now, and again at the end of session 6. They may find that their responses change as a result of the program.

Pencils
Copy of 'Dylan is being teased' x no. of participants.

15 mins **Introduction**

Participants complete sections A to E on their own and when completed, briefly share information. Emphasise any similarity between participants. Take note of any particular talents and interests that could be incorporated in the program.

Participant handbook for each participant.

30 mins **Being Happy:**

Sections A and B: Using butcher's paper, write the names of each participant at the top of a column and write on the paper for all to see, the replies of each participant.

Butcher's paper
Pens

Section C: Use a blank sheet of butcher's paper and write down the suggestions of the participants. You could draw a figure and illustrate the suggestions on the figure.

Section D: A long piece of rope is used to represent a gauge to measure the degree of feeling. Define which end is mildly happy and which end is extremely happy. Read aloud each statement and the participants stand on the point that represents their level of happiness. Briefly discuss any significant differences between participants' choices.

Length of rope

Section E: Have each word on a separate slip of paper. Distribute the slips of paper between the participants who take turns in placing each slip along the rope. Encourage discussion - participants may express differing opinions as to where a particular word belongs on the gauge. Ask the participants if they can think of any other words that express different levels of happiness and write each on a blank slip of paper and place the slip on the gauge. Take a note of the position of the slips of paper to include the gauge on the notes of the session to be distributed in the next session.

'Happy' words on slips of paper X 13

A few blank slips of paper

50 mins	**Feeling Relaxed** Section A: Continue the previous activity but this time with words that express the different levels of relaxation.	Body outline drawn on butcher's paper.
	Section B: Use butcher's paper and an outline of a person. Also demonstrate the expression of relaxation in your own body, gestures etc.	Butcher's paper and pens.
	Section C: Again on butcher's paper identify the relaxation mechanisms of each participant that they can use in the next activity.	
	Section D: Use conventional relaxation techniques, encouraging each participant to visualize the scene they associate with feeling relaxed. At the end of the relaxation practice ask each participant how they felt and to measure how relaxed they felt on a scale from one to ten.	
10 mins	**Explain the projects** Explain the projects to be completed by the next session. Encourage parent/teacher to support the participant in completing the assignments.	Participants' handbooks
5 mins	**Review** Review the main points of session one and prepare a handout to be distributed at the start of the next session. The handout includes the general points and specific examples or strategies relevant to the participants.	Handouts of key points to be prepared.

Session 2

Time	Activity	Resource
10 mins	**Key points from the previous session** Distribute the summary of the key points discovered in session 1.	Handouts of key points
20 Mins	**Discussion of project work** If there are two leaders, split the group into two groups and discuss the project work of each participant. Explain the value of the projects in encouraging a feeling of happiness.	Participants' projects
	Collect each participant's anger worksheet so that the information can be used in the current and future sessions (N.B. ensure participants have named their sheets).	Length of rope
	Place the participants' relaxation pictures along the rope.	
25 Mins	**Affective Education: Why we feel angry** A. What happens to our bodies and thinking when we feel angry? Use butcher's paper to write down the participants' suggestions for each of the 7 features. When complete discuss how anger provides energy to enable us to cope with a threat.	Butcher's paper Pens
	B. Game: Things that happen when we feel angry. Prepare two heading cards, 'Feeling angry' and 'Not feeling angry," and write each word onto smaller cards. Participants place each card in one or two columns, 'Feeling angry,' or 'Not feeling angry.'	Heading cards X 2 Angry words' cards X 34
10 Mins	**Heroes who become angry** Using butcher's paper, write down the information provided by each participant, commenting on the situations and strategies.	Butcher's paper x no. of participants
20 Mins	**A time when I have felt angry** Start by using a personal example to explain the activity. Then ask the participants to work on their own, using a sheet of butcher's paper. Provide guidance.	Butcher's paper X no. of participants. Pens

Time	Activity	Resource

20 Mins **An Emotional Tool Box to Fix the Feeling**

Briefly introduce the concept of an emotional tool box. Explain that we have different types of 'tools' to fix a feeling. These tools might be:

Physical tools	Thinking tools
Relaxation tools	Other tools
Social tools	Inappropriate tools

Resource: 2 sheets headed butcher's paper

Pens

Have two sheets of paper ready with a picture of a hammer (physical) on one and a paintbrush (relaxation) on the other. Quickly brainstorm several physical activities and methods of relaxation that could be 'tools' to fix the feeling of being angry.

Explain that the different types of 'tools' for fixing the feelings will be explored in the next session.

5 Mins **Review the key points that have been discussed during the session.**

10 Mins **Explain the Project**

Hand out the two A4 sheets of paper to each participant. Explain that they are to fill in one sheet with ideas of their own of ways to help them reduce their anger. On the other sheet they can collect ideas from their family and friends.

Resource: A4 activity sheets X 2

Set for each participant

5 Mins **Review**

Review the main points of session 2, and prepare a handout to be distributed at the start of the next session. Include the general points and specific examples or strategies relevant to participants.

Resource: Handout of key points to be prepared.

'Tools' I can use to help me feel less angry

Physical Activities

_____

_____

_____

_____

_____

_____

_____

Relaxation Activities

_____

_____

_____

_____

_____

_____

_____

'Tools' my friends or family use

Physical Activities

_____

_____

_____

_____

_____

_____

Relaxation Activities

_____

_____

_____

_____

_____

_____

Session 3

Time	Activity	Resource
5 mins	**Key points from the previous session** Distribute the summary of the key points discovered in session 2.	Handouts of key points
20 mins	**Discussion of project work** Discuss what each participant discovered about physical and relaxation tools, by themselves and from family and friends.	Participants' projects
25 mins	**A. Social Tools** The first three sections focus on how each participant could help another person who is feeling angry. In section 4, the ideas are applied to themselves. Each participant has their own list of social tools including people and how each person can help.	Butcher's paper x 4 Pens
25 mins	**B. Thinking Tools** The start of Cognitive Restructuring. Make a note of the words or strategies each participant could say to themselves. One of the thinking tools can be using one of the happiness or pleasures books created as a project after session 1.	Butcher's paper x 4 Pens
25 mins	**C. Other Tools** The special interest or hobby can be used as a relaxant, but also discuss that the amount of time involved in the interest could be too long. Consider humor - simply recalling a humorous event or seeing the funny side can be a powerful tool. Another tool is to act like someone you know who could cope well with the situation.	Butcher's paper x 4 Pens

30 mins **D. Inappropriate Tools**

This can include relieving feelings by destruction, injury, etc. The participants generate their thoughts on what are inappropriate tools and why. This can include some of the 'tools' a participant currently uses that may be inappropriate.

Butcher's paper x 4

Pens

5 mins **Project**

Explain that with parental help, each participant makes an emotional tool box and starts to practice using the tools to help fix angry feelings. The box can be a card box with a card for each type of tool or any creative design the participant and parent can make.

5 mins **Review**

Review the main points of session 3 and prepare a handout to be distributed at the start of next session. Include the general points and specific examples or strategies relevant to the participants.

Handouts of key points to be prepared

Session 4

Time	Activity	Resource
10 mins	**Key points from previous session** Distribute the summary of the key points discovered in session 3.	Handouts of key points
15 mins	**Discussion of project work** Discuss how each participant progressed in making their own emotional tool box and whether they succeeded in using some of the tools to help fix their anger feelings.	Participants' projects
20 mins	**Thermometer Activity** A. Use a length of rope as a 'thermometer' to measure the degree of feeling. With each of the situations, discuss why each of the participants have chosen a particular 'degree' of expression. Acknowledge the person who has shown the least anger and discuss how they would cope, making note of their strategies for use by the others.	Length of rope Participants' handbooks
20 mins	B. Each participant fills in their handbook. Then generate a list of all the situations that the participants find cause them anger. Use each participant's situation with all participants deciding where they would stand in the same situation. Brainstorm activities that could help the person in that situation.	Butcher's paper Pens
45 mins	**Role Play** Use role plays of each participant's situation to practice the strategies generated by the group.	
5 mins	**Project** Explain the project and distribute the butcher's paper and Post-its.	Butcher's paper and Post-its (approx. 12-15) for each participant

Time	Activity	Resource
5 mins	**Review** Review the main points of session 4 and prepare a handout to be distributed at the start of the next session Include the general points and specific examples or strategies relevant to the participants.	Handouts of key points to be prepared

Session 5

Time	Activity	Resource
10 mins	**Key points from previous session** Distribute the summary of the key points discovered in session 4.	Handouts of key points
20 mins	**Discussion of project work** Discuss each person's thermometer and the strategies they have used since the last session.	Participants' projects
45 mins	**Social Stories™** Explain how to write a Social Story™ using examples based on the participants' list of situations that create a feeling of anger. (session 4, 3b).	List of situations that cause anger.
15 mins	**Antidote to poisonous thoughts** A. Ask the group to decide whether the following list of thoughts are helpful or unhelpful. Have each statement on a separate piece of paper and construct two lists (Helpful and Unhelpful).	Statement cards x 16

I'm a loser
I can stay calm
I'm not good at homework
I can't get it to work
Relaxing makes my thinking better
Good decision
The teacher will be pleased if I stay calm
Think then choose
They will laugh at me
I have friends that are kind
It's not winning it's enjoying the game
Everyone hates me
I will be better next time
I am going to show how mature I am
I could get hurt
Relax, it's only words

20 mins	B. Brainstorm the participants' ideas and add to the list of antidotes to poisonous thoughts.	

Time	Activity	Resource
5 mins	**Project** Explain the project.	
5 mins	**Review** Review the main points of session 5 and prepare a handout to be distributed at the start of the next session. Include general points and specific examples or strategies relevant to the participants.	Handouts of key points to be prepared

Session 6

Time	Activity	Resource
10 mins	**Key points from previous session** Distribute the summary of the key points discovered in session 5.	Handouts of key points
10 mins	**Discussion of project work** Discuss each person's Social Story™ and list of antidotes to poisonous thoughts.	Participants' Social Stories™ and antidotes
40 mins	**Strategies** Participants can work in pairs through sections 3, 4, 5 and 6, to design a program for each other. Allocate 20 minutes for each person.	Paper Pens
25 mins	Review program strategies as a whole group activity.	
15 mins	**Conclusion** Ask participants to brainstorm the key points they have learn from the course.	Butcher's paper
15 mins	Distribute 'Dylan is being teased.'	'Dylan is being teased' copy for each participant. Pencils
5 mins	Distribute certificates	Certificate of participation for each participant